This document details my seven day trip to Iceland from June 13th through June 19th in 2019.

Thank you to Hideshi for encouraging me to document this adventure. I hope that fathers around the world can bond through exploration of their warrior spirits.

I left San Jose International Airport on Wednesday morning, stopping in Denver and Newark before flying to Reykjavik.

In Newark, I met Jorge who also gave me a ride from the airport. We arrived in Reykjavik around 10am. He took me to the Blue Lagoon for a few minutes to check out and then took me to the KEX Hostel which cost me $90 for two nights.

I went to Skal for dinner.

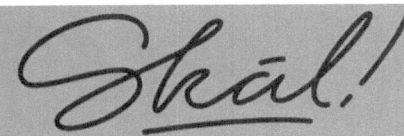

MATUR

Tilvalið til þess að deila

Réttirnir eru afgreiddir þegar þeir eru klárir

SNAKK

kryddaðar MÖNDLUR (VG)	350 kr
grillað súrdeigs BRAUÐ og kryddsmjör (V)	400 kr
HUMMUS & sölkex (VG)	750 kr

SMÆRRI

kramdar KARTÖFLUR, blóðbergssalt & graslauksmajó (VG)	650 kr
*reyktar GULRÆTUR, brennd sítróna, piparrót, soya, söl & dill (VG)	1450 kr
gratineraður GEITAOSTUR, fennel kex & rabbabara sulta (V)	1450 kr
**krydduð SELJURÓT, ostakrem, sýrt selleri & kóriander (V)	1450 kr
ferskt BOK CHOI með ricotta, kerfil & límónu (V)	1450 kr
*sýrðir smá TÓMATAR í sætu basilediki & ferskostur (V)	1550 kr
NAUTA TARTAR, ostakrem, rauðrófugljái, súrar & fennelkex	1750 kr
brenndur BLEIKJU TARTAR, agúrkur, engifer & sesam	1750 kr

PYLSA/BULSA með öllu!

remúlaði, steiktur, tómatssósa, mustarður & sýrðar gúrkur	1000 kr
COMBO: PYLSA/BULSA (VG) + bríó + prins póló	2000 kr

STÆRRI

SELJURÓTAR & möndlusteik, epli, brennd sítróna & agúrkur (VG)	2000 kr
bökuð BLEIKJA, caperssmjör, möndlur & kartöflumús	2350 kr
kryddaðar GRÍSA KINNAR, stappaðar kartöflur, epli & fennel kex	2350 kr
beinlaus LAMBARIF, rabbabara BBQ, reykt súrmjólk & seljurót	2450 kr
NAUTA skirt steik, kryddsmjör, kartöflur & sýrt selleri	2500 kr

SÆTT

ÁSTARPUNGAR, mysingskaramella & kardimommusykur (V)	1000 kr
SKYR & hvítsúkkulaði, hvönn, hafrar & rabbabarakrap	1300 kr

GRÆNMETISRÉTTUR

VEGAN RÉTTUR

DRYKKUR

Gleðistund 14.00 - 18.00

Bríó 750kr - Húsvín glas 1250kr - Kranastél 1500kr

BJÓR Á KRANA - 0,2L / 0,4L

BRÍÓ (pilsner)	1000 kr
ÚLFRÚN (session ipa)	1300 kr
SÓLVEIG (hoppy weizen)	1400 kr
bjór VIKUNNAR (spyrjið)	SJÁ Á KRANA
árstíðabundinn BORG BJÓR (spyrjið)	1000/1700 kr
bjór frá SMÁBRUGGHÚSUM (spyrjið)	1000/1700 kr

Á FLÖSKU

SULTASLAKUR (íslenskur rabarbara & epla cíder)	3500 kr
lífrænn EPLACIDER (700 ml)	5000 kr

KRANASTÉL

REYKJAVÍK MULE, vodka, brennivín, engiferlímonaði & skessujurt	1750 kr

LÍFRÆNN VERMÚT

wermut ERBORISTA, rauður	1500 kr

NÁTTÚRUVÍN - GLAS / FLASKA

succés cuca de llum TREPAT (rautt)	1600 / 7200 kr
succés experiéncia PARELLADA (hvítt)	1600 / 7200 kr

Við erum alltaf með fleiri flöskur opnar fyrir glasavín, spyrðu okkur!

FLASKA

PESECKÁ leánka (hvítt)	7200 kr
Lulu Berlue 2017 CABERNET SAUVIGNION (rósa)	8700 kr
Megalodon SYRAH (rautt)	8700 kr
Volcanic PINOT GRIS (hvítt)	8700 kr
ormiale 2013 MERLOT & CABERNET SAUVIGNON (rautt)	10900 kr

ANNAÐ

skál LÍMONAÐI	550 kr
skál birki KOMBUCHA	750 kr
pepsi, pepsi max, appelsín, engifer öl & sódavatn	350 kr

* Borið fram með grilluðu súrdeigsbrauði

**Hægt að gera vegan

Tilkynnið okkur ef um ofnæmi sé að ræða

Finnið okkur @skalrvk og taggið okkur #skalrvk

The meal cost $57 and I left this 5 star review on Google.

"A little pricey but delicious meal. I ordered the goat cheese with fennel crackers followed by skirt steak with herb potatoes and celery. The chef preparing the meal took great pride in his work. Also, I was happy to see a larger size amount of protein within the meal. In other words, there was a nice balance between steak and potatoes. To describe the dessert, I would say I was pleasantly surprised and delighted to see such creativity. Disappointed that skyr, white chocolate and rhubarb granata is a common icelandic favorite, creativity may be taken away but definitely not the flavor."

From there, headed back to the hostel to rest. I walked around the city, checking out the shops, the ocean and a famous church.

I tried a skyr pancake and was not a fan.

The next morning, I went to rent a car. The rental cost $214 to use 5 days or $43 per day. I ended up paying $75 for an international driver's license as well but did not need it in Iceland. The IDL is a good thing to order several months in advance as AAA might have sold this to me for much less (it turns out I never need this IDL).

By the way, I also picked up some things for charging my Fitbit and phone. My phone was essential for GPS and I would often use airplane mode to conserve battery.

I drove to the Lava Tunnel, which I thought was a great tour for $5. It turns out this was actually $54. The Lava Tunnel seemed to be one of those overpriced tourist attractions. The caves did not have many unique features like the bat caves I have seen in the United States (Carlsbad Caverns and Mt Shasta Caverns).

The tour was pretty short, maybe an hour or so. There were a few interesting structures.

After the Lava Tunnel, I headed to the Silfra Meeting Point. Lupin were planted in Iceland to help with the sandstorms.

I expected to see a waterfall in Selfoss based on Google. However, I only saw this bridge. Please do not add generic photos of Iceland to specific cities because travellers will go to those cities looking for those places in the photos!

I tried a bunch of chocolate on my drive. Sukkuladi Med Kaffibragdi. Sukkuladi means chocolate. I passed some time on my drive speaking out Sukkuladi Med Kaffibragdi but pretending it meant something exciting, shocking or sad by enunciating the syllables differently.

Close to the Silfra meeting point was Oxrarfoss. Foss means falls!

Silfra is a place where you can snorkel between two continents, North America and Europe, as Iceland is a part of both. Another fun fact is that Iceland is 11% ice, whereas Greenland is 80% ice. Go figure.

The tour cost $126. We waited while everyone got dressed, then waited more to explain the safety rules, then waited for other tour groups to move through the water before we could get in.

I gave this 2 star review on Google.

"I would not recommend snorkeling here on the tour. It is a glorified lazy river. Swimming between two continents seems cool but there is just no life. I saw one fish and others could not see any for weeks. Mind you, I am a freediver with a two minute breath hold so staying on the surface and not having a weight belt I felt 100% restricted. Underwater, there is 30 meters of visibility but you cant even dive down to the bottom. The dry suits were nice and I did stay pretty dry with minimal water leaking in only because I was doing somersaults in the water out of boredom."

Apparently several drownings occurred due to heart attacks from the cold water, so the tour is really restrictive.

Have you ever been on a tour where you felt like you were being processed? Anytime, I feel that way, even in a restaurant, the experience is negatively impacted. In some cases, people take a canned photo. There were so many photos online, I did not even find mine after ten minutes of searching but here is what you could expect, one foot on North America, one hand on Europe.

I left as quickly as possible to drive to Strokker geyser. This geyser erupts every few minutes.

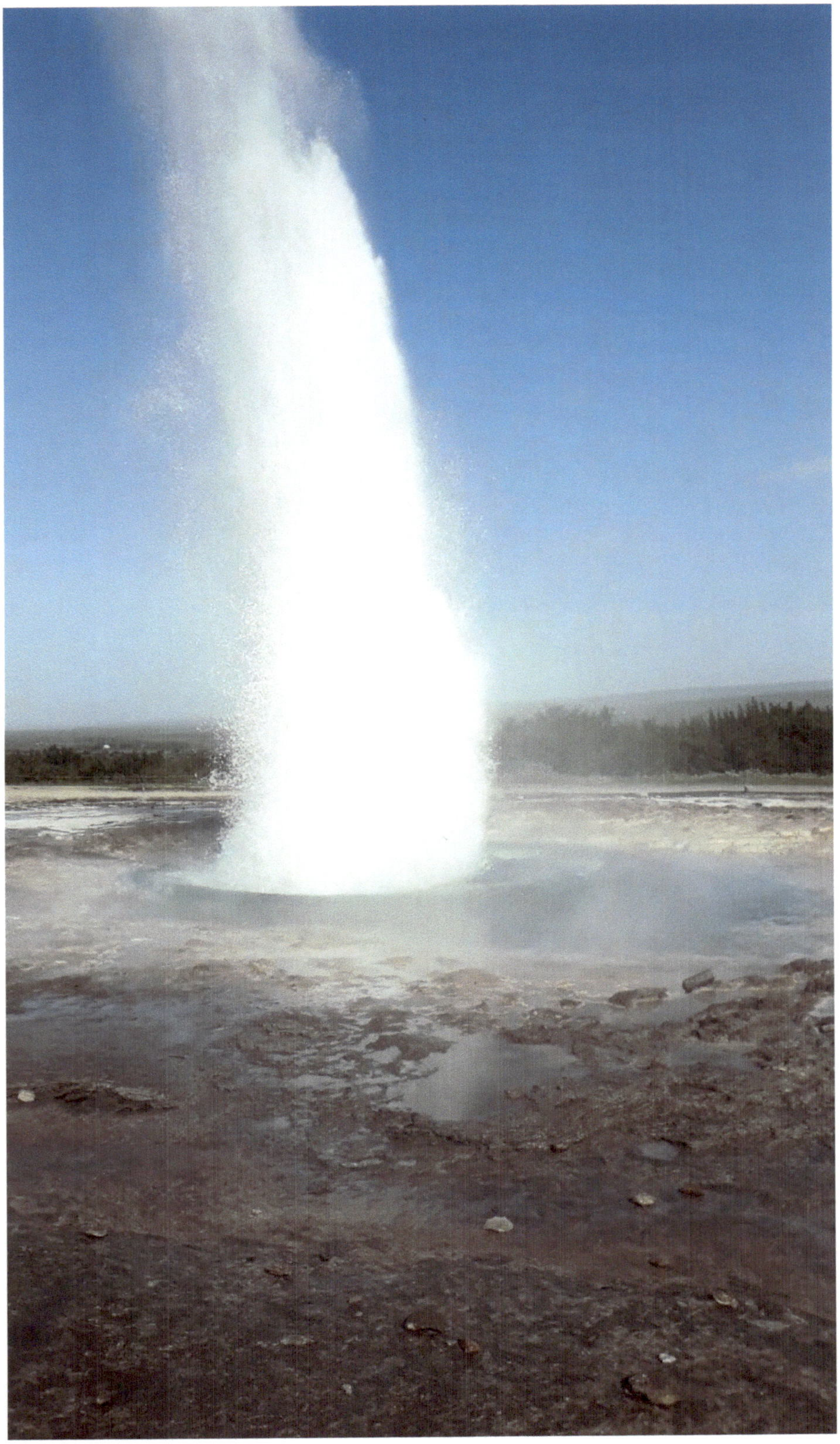

To hike around the area is less than a mile one way. There are several pools and some nice views.

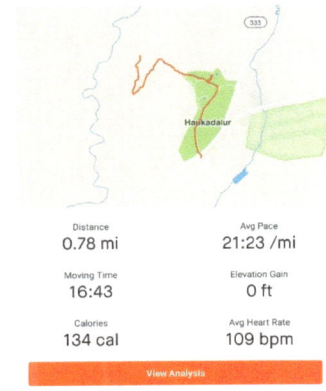

Distance	Avg Pace
0.78 mi	21:23 /mi
Moving Time	Elevation Gain
16:43	0 ft
Calories	Avg Heart Rate
134 cal	109 bpm

View Analysis

I left this 5 star review on Google.

"This is a great place to hike. There are many natural hot springs. Though they are prohibited to get in, they are beautiful. Strokker blows every few minutes and its relaxing to just watch for half an hour. It is touristy, but the grounds are kept very nice."

My next stop was Gulfoss or Golden Falls. This was probably my favorite of all the Iceland waterfalls. I appreciate the power and varying levels. 5 stars.

I found myself at Urrioafoss at 3am, yet its was still light out. Iceland never got dark while I was here between June 13th through June 19th. Apparently, the opposite occurs in some fjords like Seydisfjordur, where it might be dark for 3 months during the winter.

I loved being here alone. The river and waterfall were wide, bustling with activity and then, just around the bend, it was peaceful as can be.

On the third day, my plan was to check out three waterfalls and maybe an ice cave or glacier and then head to my hostel in East Iceland for two nights.

I went to Gluggafoss first. Another 5 star waterfall. I think there were 5 waterfalls that I ranked 5 stars.

Next, was Seljalandsfoss. This place was covered with tourists and I was not impressed. However, there was a main falls and then several trickling falls which were nice. I left this 3 star Google review.

"Beautiful falls but tons of tourists. Hard to give it a higher rating when you have gullfoss, urrioafoss and gluggafoss to compare to."

The next falls was Skogafoss. It started out as a hike to the top which was really short.

Then, I started to follow a trail that kept leading to more and more waterfalls.

I added the picture above and below to Google as Bridge Falls. It marks roughly 5 miles from Skogar and there are pretty much no falls after that. Well there are, but the hike changes into what I consider the second of four parts to the hike.

Scott Izu
June 16, 2019 at 10:14 AM

Morning Run

Distance	Pace	Time
4.97 mi	16:10 /mi	1h 20m

The path then turns into a fire road. At this point, I really did not know where I was hiking. I saw signs for Basar and Fimmvorduhals. I did not know what either was but I was filled with a rush by what I had just hiked and hoped to explore even more. I love water!

The fog started to kick in. It was slightly drizzling. "Maybe I am in over my head. As long as I stay dry and weather does not get worse, I should be fine," I thought. However, I had no

gear, just a long sleeve running shirt, a sweater, a wind breaker, jeans and some running shoes. "If my feet get too wet, I will have to turn back and these running shoes are not helping to keep water out.", I thought. I had no water but had been drinking from the streams. I will drink from streams with rocks and rapidly flowing water that serve as natural filters but only in certain places. Mt Shasta City Park and this trail are two such places. I will not even drink water from Yosemite. In other words, I check with the locals as well as use my own intuition.

So, there I was, hiking on a rocky road, unprepared with only the thought that I could run back in an emergency if the weather changed. I have done two half marathons this year. I practiced running with minimal water and replenishment to prepare. Also, I am used to regulating my body temperature, which I use to regularly swim in Santa Cruz's 50° F water. I can build an emergency shelter if necessary which I learned when earning my Eagle Scout award. I just add this information as context so others can gauge their survival instincts before doing anything dangerous.

As the weather continued to worsen and not really knowing where I was or where I was going, I seriously considered just turning back. The problem with not knowing where one is going is that even a 1 mile hike can become a 3 mile hike as one zig zags, back tracks, and navigates around various rivers and mountain terrain. I was still on the fire road. This lasted for a good hour or so and I had not seen a single person for several hours.

Finally, a warden drove up the fireroad. "Are you okay?" "Are you cold?" "Please stop by and having coffee before you head up."

He continued driving and I told him I could hike the half mile to his emergency hut. I was reenergized knowing I was not alone out there. When I got to their hut, the fog was so thick and it was so windy and cold that I opted to stay. There was no way I would get to my hostel in Egilsstadir. It cost about $55 and he provided me with plenty of ham, bread, cheese and water. He also gave me some coffee, an emergency sleeping bag and a cozy mat. I was more comfortable there then when I go camping back home. He also called me crazy.

Another couple was in the hut when I arrived. They told me about Porsmork, Basar and Landigalur. They also talked about Eyjafjalljokull and Myrdalsjokull. Lastly, Fimmvorduhals. The warden gave me a few pages to read about the Fimmvorduhals trekking trail. I decided I wanted to go to Porsmork and on Google, it showed as a different place than Basar, so I did not realize until much later that Basar is in Porsmork.

Jokull means glacier. It turns out I was about to hike on the snow between two glaciers! The hut was Baldvinsskali Hut. If I had planned better for this 30 mile hike, I would have marked Bridge Falls (which I added to Google), Balvinsskali Hut, Fimmvorduhals and Basar on Google

Maps before the hike. However, this was completely spontaneous and I was ready to turn around in an emergency.

It was about 11pm when I arrived and I left Skogar sometime after 5pm. I took a power nap, woke up at 3am and saw the fog had cleared. I knocked on the warden's cabin door and tried to wake him up as politely as possible. Based on the new information, a normal hiking pace would take 4 hours to get to Porsmork, 4 hours back and 4 hours to Skogar. I would get back by 3pm, which would kill my Sunday plans. Also, I was told a bus might take me from Basar to Skogar, so that was an option.

I asked the warden for some more food so I could head out. The weather was chilly and this was the start of my hike in the snow, which I consider the third of four sections of this hike. There were large posts in the ground and from each post I could find the next one, although sometimes it was not easy. Sometimes I would go the wrong direction at a fork in the road. I hiked across altering terrains of snow and black mountain. In some places the mountain terrain was slippery. The snow was not deep, so it was fairly easy to walk through although some places I had to kick in foot holds to avoid slipping. I fell in a few places but did not get injured.

Avalanches and snow breaking through were concerns so I followed known tracks. There were plenty of footprints in the ground, although I would not see anyone until I arrived at Basar.

Luckily, deep snow, was not an issue. Once in Mt Shasta, I tried hiking to Upper Mcloud Falls in deep snow. Every step, my leg dropped until snow reached my knees. After only .5 miles, my son and I were exhausted and turned back. We later came back with snowshoes and completed the hike.

Injury is another big concern in the wilderness. Injury would change this fun hike into a survival exercise.

After some time, I came to Modi and Magdlni, two volcanic craters, which were created from the 2010 volcanic eruption.

Shortly after this, I came to the fourth leg of the hike. The terrain was once again foggy and reminiscent of the Lord of the Rings. Steep mountain regions where one small mistake and I could slip to my death. Here was one of the more dangerous crossings, followed by a scenic view as I made it out of the fog and down to Porsmork.

After wandering around, trying to find a way to get to Porsmork as marked on Google Maps, I walked up and down the river next to Basar until finally giving up. In Basar, I discovered that I was already in Basar, which is in Porsmork!

I had no idea how long I had hiked until I saw this sign.

It was now 6am, one hour ahead of schedule. The bus would not come to Basar until 6:30pm and it did not even go directly to Skogar. I would have to hike back! As I started my hike I snapped a picture of what I thought was Porsmork at the time and finally ran into some fellow hikers!

With the fog cleared, I also got some better pictures of the glaciers and Modi/Magni.

Walking back I started to feel faint and wondered why I had so little energy. I was hitting a wall. I told myself I would not eat my bread, cheese and ham until 9am. I pulled the food out only to find I only had bread! The cheese and ham had both crumbled into small bits in my sweater pouch. I ate every little crumb I could find in my sweater knowing I was low on energy. After doing so, I discovered that I was really hungry. This gave me the boost I needed and I found myself again jogging along the snow. I needed to maintain good time to keep my feet dry as well as escape various conditions.

I made it back to the Balvinsskali hut by 8:40am. I ate and drank to refuel. I rested for 20 minutes and asked for toilet paper and a Snickers bar for the road. Snickers provide tons of calories which can be good for lightweight fuel. Some marathon runners carry Snickers bars.

Did I mention, I had to poop a lot on this hike? I stopped three times to do the deed. In one instance, I used leaves to clean myself and wiped my hands on wet grass until I could rinse more thoroughly in a stream. Toilet paper is much nicer. Wipe, fold. Wipe, fold. Get one last wipe if you can.

I am a clean freak and at scout camp one year, I did not go to the bathroom for a whole week just to avoid the outhouse. Another year, I am embarrassed to say that I pooped in a garbage can to avoid the outhouse. As I grew older, I became more comfortable adapting. Although I still think it is gross, there is some psychological chain broken as I force myself to adapt as I connect to nature.

Making great time, I caught up to the couple I met the night before in the hut about a mile before we reached Skogar.

From Basar to Skogar, I made great time. According to Strava, I did one segment, placing 5th in the world! Of course, this only compares to other Strava users.

I use my Fitbit to record an activity and it gives me real time pace information. It directly syncs with Strava. I can also record directly on the Strava app for my phone. I did this below for my return trip, which I mistakenly recorded as a bike activity (which I can change) and named Sklogafoss to Basar (which I can also change). It should be a hike from Basar to Skogar.

Scott Izu
Today at 5:49 AM

Sklogafoss to Basar

Distance	Elevation Gain
14.93 mi	3,347 ft
Moving Time	Avg Power
5:20:25	57 W
Avg Speed	Calories
2.8 mi/h	1,224 cal

View Analysis

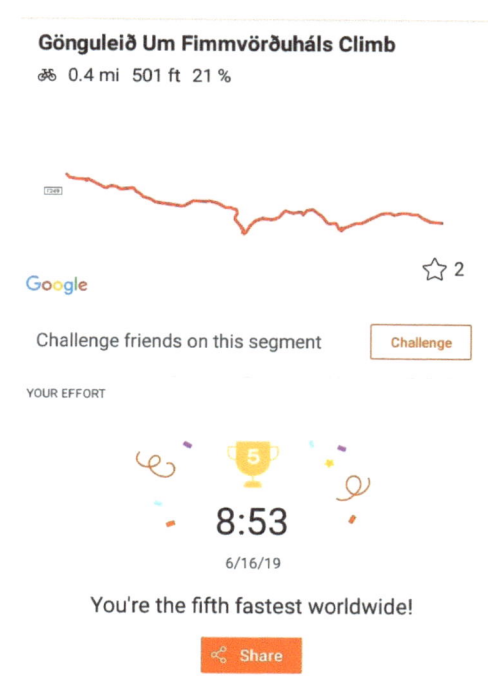

Gönguleið Um Fimmvörðuháls Climb
0.4 mi   501 ft   21 %

Google   ☆ 2

Challenge friends on this segment   Challenge

YOUR EFFORT

🏆 5
8:53
6/16/19

You're the fifth fastest worldwide!

Share

The end of my 30 mile hike led me into the next day. It was 12pm when I got back and it would be 2 hours to drive to Glacier Lagoon. I wasted time trying to shower and eat at Skogar. There were so many people. The showers only accepted coins which I wasted time hiking up to the restaurant to obtain, only to find the shower machines were not working.

I left to go to the nearest swimming pool which was in Viks. I showered there and soaked for a bit to recover. As I left Viks, it was now nearing 2pm. People said that ice caves were all melted during the summer but I vaguely remember some tour in Viks. As I left Viks, I decided I would not make it to Glacier Lagoon in time for a tour. I discovered online that the ice cave tours all met at the Vik Ice Bistro (or Ice Cafe or Ice Restaurant). I went back to Vik to see if any tour had an extra spot I could hop on.

I found one group which was full but they mentioned another guide would be back. Soon, I was talking with another person who explained that I need to wait a while as Iceland phone service connects. He also said I need to prefix phone numbers with + or 00 and 354. So I called 00-354-588-1358 which is Arctic Adventures. He helped me navigate the tour's online site which was not very good as some buttons did not work on my phone.

The 3pm tour had 5 spots available. I took one spot for $158. The tour was a 45 minute ride to the base of Myrdalsjokull which is a glacier on the Katla volcano. Unlike other ice caves, this one was on a volcano which was cool. That caused a unique ice and lava sand combination. Like any tour, we were kinda rushed through the cave. I purposely went last and moved quickly so it appeared as if I was always waiting for the people in front of me. The tour guide appreciated that and let me go behind him some of the time to take pictures because he knew I would not slow the group down.

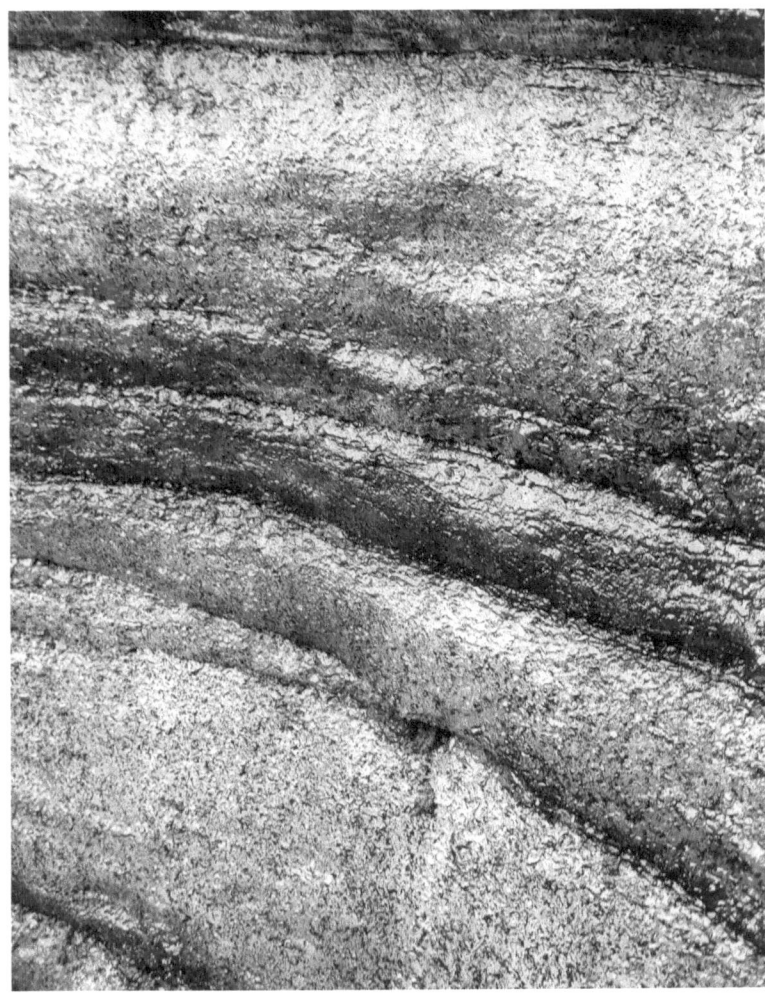

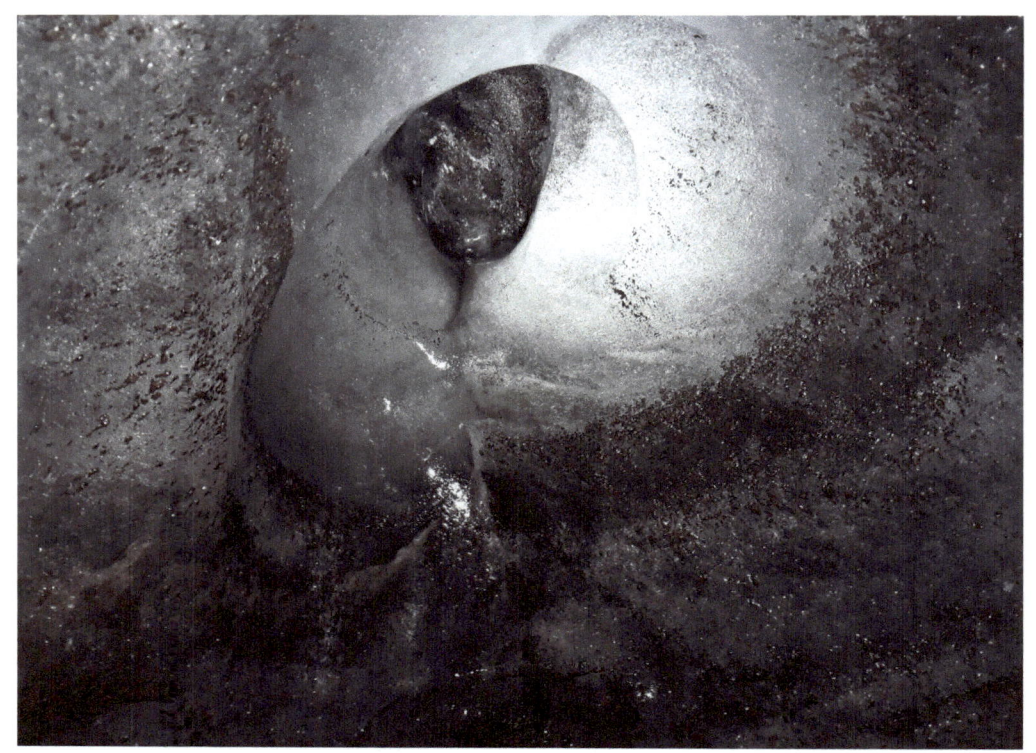

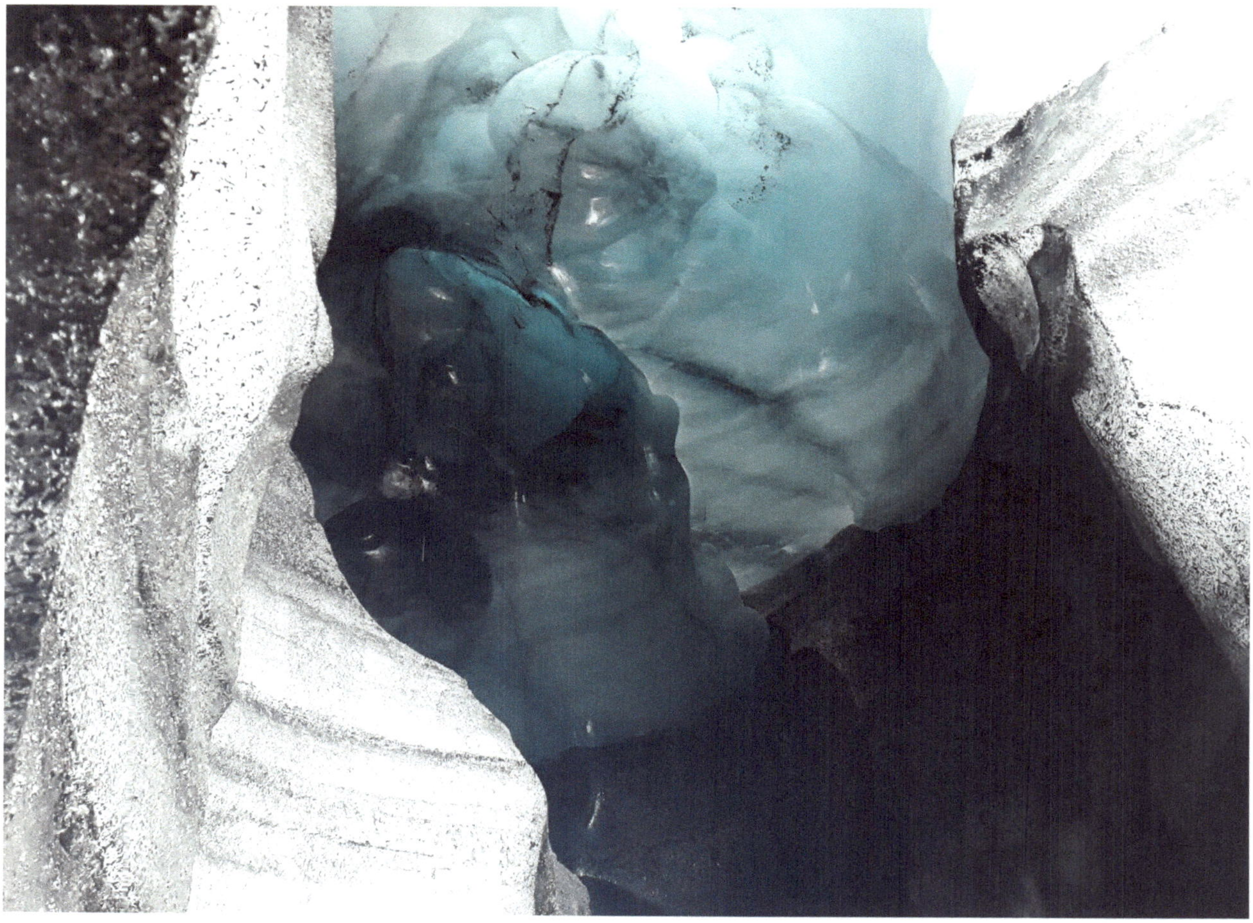

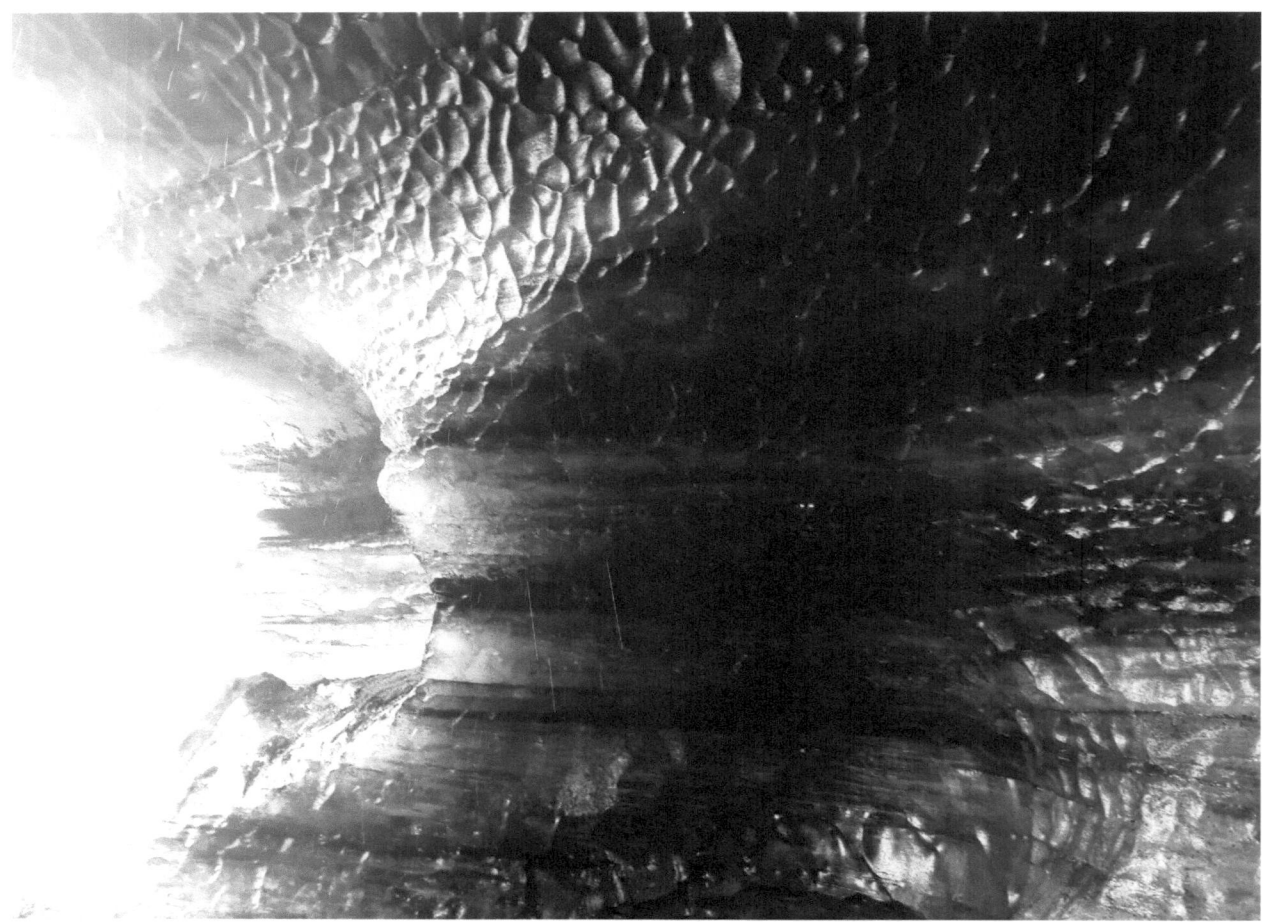

The tour guide was very nice. Although, in general, I do not like tours. I take a few here and there to learn. Typically, I think tours are rushed with little time to explore. Also, people are generally herded like cattle, which never feels good. The biggest benefit I see is obtaining the knowledge the tour guide has. I will be that somewhat annoying person in the group asking tons of questions. I also asked about other places in Iceland that were not related to the tour.

The tour guide is hawkthebeard on instagram and also does different tours like ski mobile tours.

I discovered that the tour guide loved scuba diving. He talked about how much better Silfra is when you can go down to the bottom. He also talked about spearfishing. Spearfishing is illegal in iceland. Hand held line and rods are allowed and you do not even need a permit. Hawaiian slings and spearguns are considered automatic triggers. Additional gear or equipment is not allowed.

We returned around 5pm and I went to Smidjan Bruggus. I gave this place a 5 star for the delicious burger, fries and local brew. This micro brewery was a recommendation from the tour guide. I actually got a small discount and the meal cost me $28.

Unfortunately, I still would not make it out to my hostel for the second night. I paid for two nights and completely wasted nearly $150. I decided rather than rush, I would book no more hostels and just sleep in the rental car.

I went to Svartifoss which has 5 falls, a few of which I added to Google.

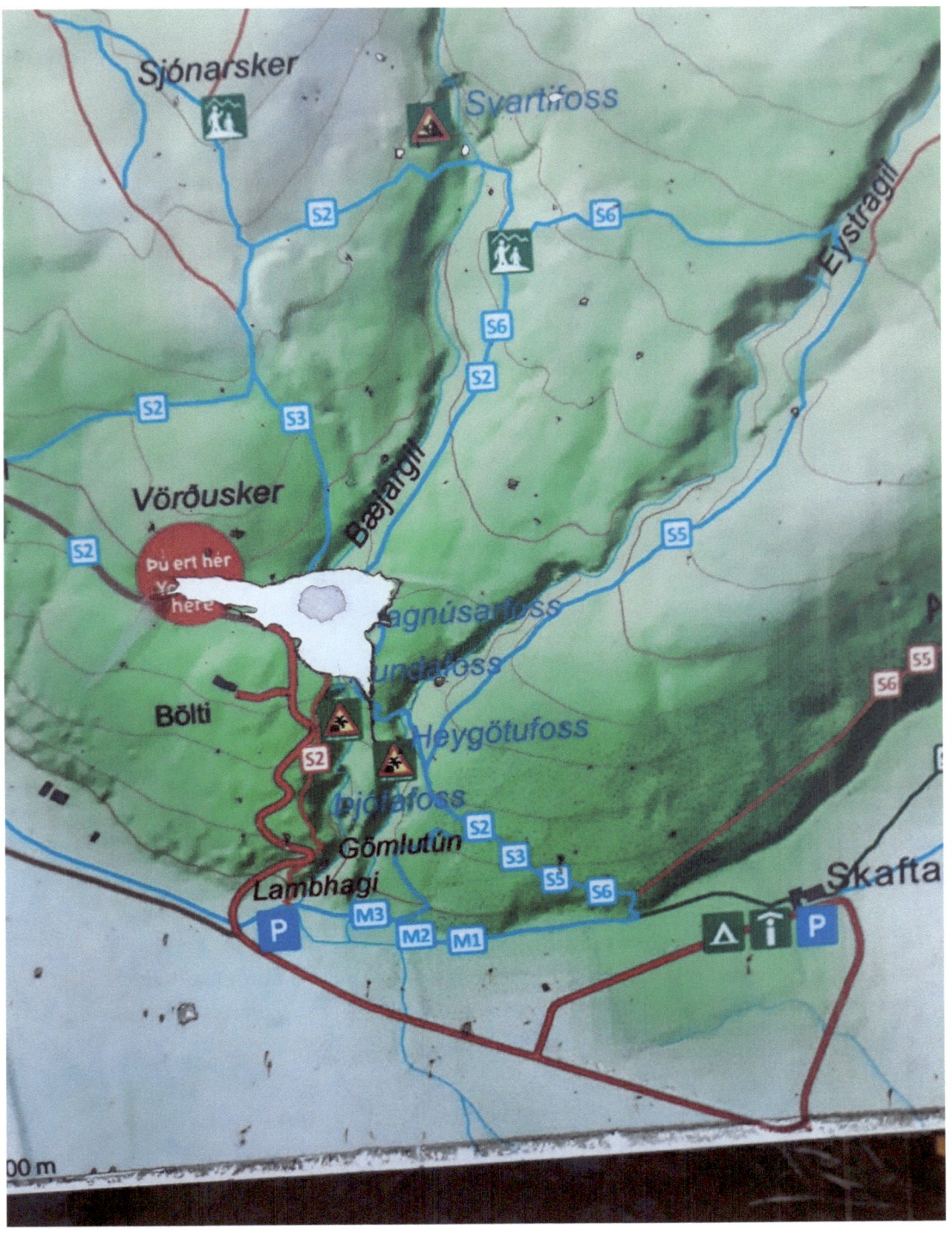

This is a nice waterfall and has unique basalt columns.

My next stop was Svinafellsjokull, which is a glacier. The route was somewhat rough terrain and I wish rented a jeep rather than the Toyota Taurius.

I wanted to hike all the way to touch the glacier and maybe even hike on it. This was probably the most scary part of my trip. I climbed down some rock faces to try to get to the glacier but could not.

With broken rocks as terrain, tracking the paths of other people is a lot harder. Sometimes, water runoff creates paths which might look like a trail at first sight, although collection of debris can highlight the difference. Hiking along the water line can sometimes be advantageous if it exposes terrain with good grip. On the other hand, loose gravel, debris, moisture and mud can make water lines harder to use.

At any moment, avalanche and slipping were real threats. Falling into the water here would mean minutes before hypothermia would set in. There were cliffs at the water's edge so getting out would be difficult. Even if lucky enough to get out, getting back to a place to regain warmth quickly would be another challenge. I decided to head back since I did not have a guide. The risk was just too great for me.

I headed out to Glacier Lagoon and Diamond Beach.

I pulled over on the side of the road to sleep around 4am. Each day in Iceland, it was hard to go to sleep before 4am because it stayed light out and there were so many amazing places. There are many backpackers and campers so sleeping in the car on the side of the road was fairly easy.

The next day, I got up a little bummed that I could not spearfish and fishing was likely out of the question since it was a Monday and I only had two days left before flying out on Wednesday. I had not seen any fish despite stopping by lakes, rivers and bridges (except fish under 6 inches long). As I was driving, suddenly, I saw the solo angler, tackling the lake all by himself.

I am drawn to that determination and focus. I have had days where I have caught 13 trout and days where I have spent 8 hours only to come up empty handed. Try new things, hone my craft, learn from the masters. I pulled over.

I watched the man at work and within ten minutes the beautiful pveit lake produces a nice brown trout using a bobber, foot long leader and shrimp as bait. He let me check out his rig and do a few casts. Apparently, I got a few bites, although with trout, the bite is so subtle, it can be confused with snagging a log or grass.

The man was chief of a cod fishery. It was Iceland's national independence day and he said fishing was better than cleaning the house. He said he caught 30 fish in a day but no one was interested in taking his fish. He offered me the fish and suggested I buy a disposable one time use barbeque that can be found at any gas station. For a guy like me, grilling a freshly caught fish by the beach or lake is a dream come true. I ate this fish with fresh carrots that I bought from a Bonus grocery store.

Driving to the eastern fjords, the country is beautiful. The drive takes a good nine hours to get back to Reykjavik, so it is debatable whether it is worth it. Going through Southern Iceland, there is plenty to see on the trip and several hours of return time tend to accumulate quickly.

Stopping in Seydisfjordur, the restaurant I visited was out of cod, no boat tours were running and the information station was vacant. I opted to have a local lager, enjoy the view for a bit and headed to my next destination, unimpressed. Here, is where consulting a local would have been helpful as I did not get to do much in the fjords.

I did pick up a hitchhiker, one of many out of country workers who fly in for the summer and winter tourist seasons. Iceland's big money maker is now tourism, followed by fishing. Just a few years ago, fishing was number one.

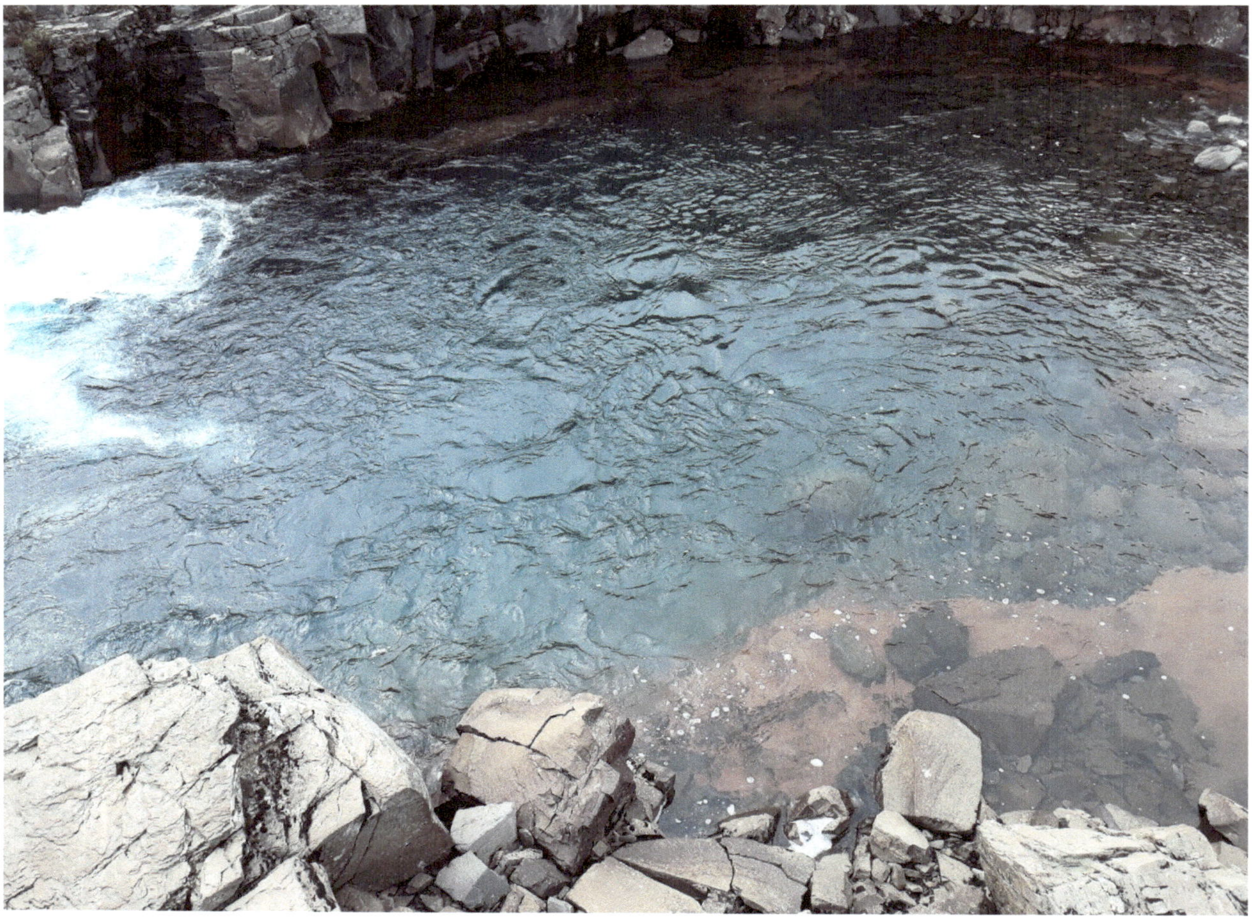

I arrived at the Storuro hiking trail around 9pm. It seemed like there were many trails heading up to Storuro. However, it was very hard to find any. The ground was rocky, half of it was covered with snow and there were footprints all over the place. I decided to just make my best guess to follow paths and footprints up. I would be fairly certain I was way off course but would run into footprints again. I followed my phone's GPS, put my phone in airplane mode and turned on my fitbit. I made tracking marks every .2 miles to see where I was. At one point, footprints led into the snow but were then covered up by the snow.

I made a staircase by digging small footholds into the snow and slid down a couple times. It was about 15 ft high. Fun and crazy!

I just continued up the mountain but the terrain was not great and it was foggy. I did not want to just walk across ice because I did not know where ponds were. Despite these obstacles, I slowly made way toward Storuro over the next hour.

I finally found a marker from another trail that led to Storuro. I used this to hike the rest of the way.

When I came to 500 ft away from Storuro, based on my phone's GPS, I saw this. It's hard to see but looked to me like 1/4 mile covered in snow and ice.

On the way back down, I slid down thin patches of ice to get down quickly. By the time I got to the road, I had lost my car. I walked down the road, then changed my mind thinking it would be better to walk up first, then down, if I did not see my car. After hiking up a way, I hiked back down. Wet, cold and nearly 11pm, I found my car.

Run

Scott Izu
June 17, 2019 at 6:25 PM

Storuro Hike

Distance	Elevation Gain
5.13 mi	1,879 ft
Moving Time	Avg Pace
1:52:26	21:54 /mi
Calories	Avg Heart Rate
1,757 cal	125 bpm

View Analysis

I went to Ja Sael and ordered two dinners, the pan fried cod and the lamb cheeseburger. With dessert, this cost me $62.

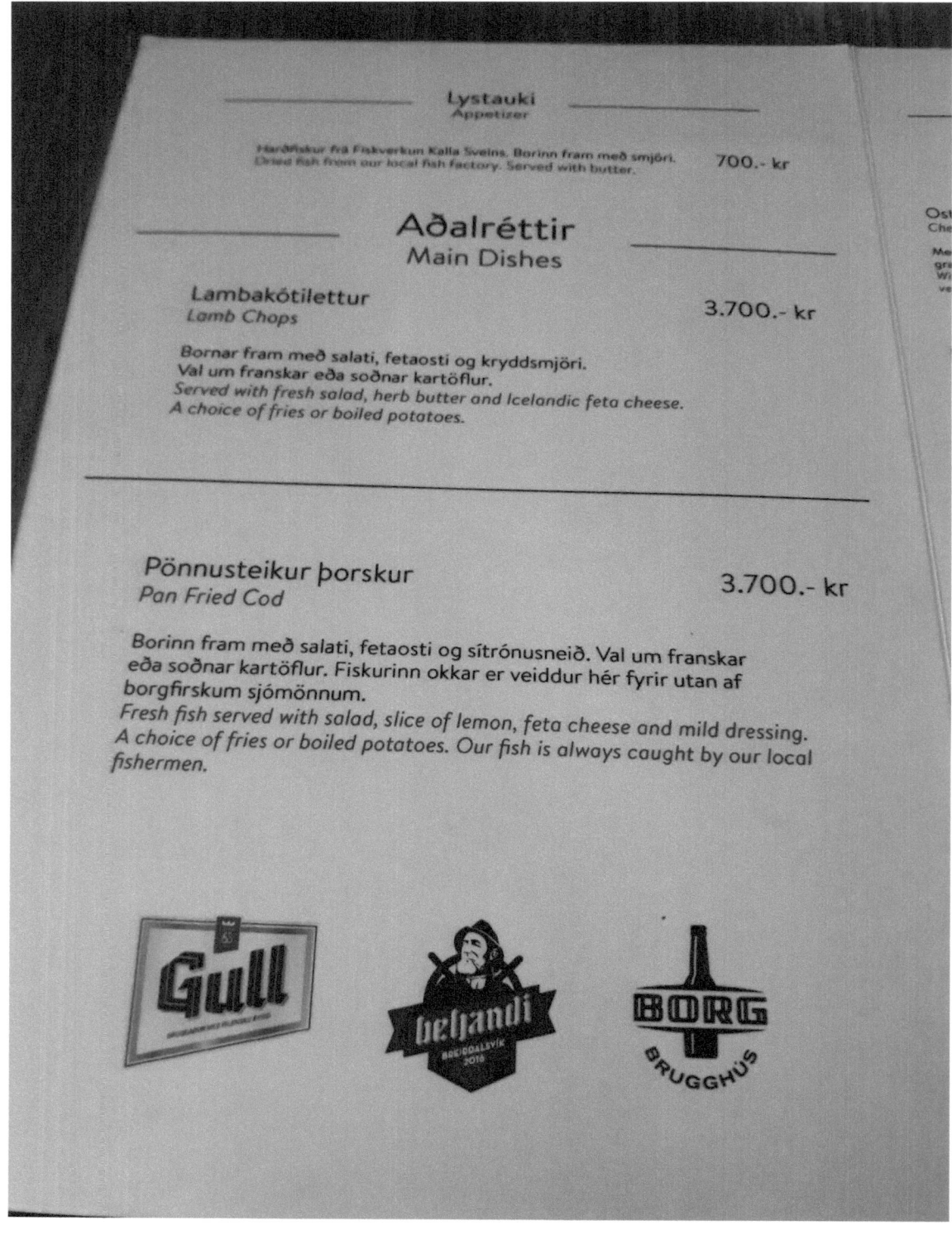

Lystauki
Appetizer

Harðfiskur frá Fiskverkun Kalla Sveins. Borinn fram með smjöri.   700.- kr
Dried fish from our local fish factory. Served with butter.

Aðalréttir
Main Dishes

Lambakótilettur
Lamb Chops   3.700.- kr

Bornar fram með salati, fetaosti og kryddsmjöri.
Val um franskar eða soðnar kartöflur.
Served with fresh salad, herb butter and Icelandic feta cheese.
A choice of fries or boiled potatoes.

Pönnusteikur þorskur
Pan Fried Cod   3.700.- kr

Borinn fram með salati, fetaosti og sítrónusneið. Val um franskar
eða soðnar kartöflur. Fiskurinn okkar er veiddur hér fyrir utan af
borgfirskum sjómönnum.
Fresh fish served with salad, slice of lemon, feta cheese and mild dressing.
A choice of fries or boiled potatoes. Our fish is always caught by our local
fishermen.

I gave the restaurant 5 stars even though I did not think the food was spectacular. In fact, it reminded me a little of the standard meal you might have at a kid's birthday party with friends over the summer. You know, the simple cheeseburger or chicken served with a store bought house salad.

This was my Google review.

"I ordered the pan fried cod and was hungry after a day of driving and hiking so also got the cheeseburger and dessert. The cod was not anything special, nor was the burger. The first batch of fries came out too salty, I forgot to order sweet potato fries for the second batch and my request to lighten up on the salt was met with zero seasoning on the second batch. The dessert was chocolate cake with skyr (I think). I am not a big fan of skyr. I think Iceland is all too expensive and in general, I did not like icelandic food. My friends say I'm hard to please. Despite all this, I loved the meal. I love eating fresh cod (they gave me plenty of cod) caught by local fisherman and a cheeseburger with lamb, made from local farmers. This is the Icelandic livelihood and I feel honored and special to experience a piece of it. My IPA was also brewed locally."

After dinner, I drove to the Borgarfjardarhreppur harbor (hofn) and spent a brief time checking out the Puffins. It was late, cold and windy but they had a bird viewing station. I also saw many beautiful birds throughout the week. Apparently, I arrived just in time for the birds to come back to settle in for the night.

I ended the day sleeping on the side of a country road (in the rental car, of course).

Due to time restraints, I had to deprioritize Myvatan Nature Baths (which I did drive past), Eyjafjordur, Dynjandi and Kirkjufell. The Myvatan Nature Baths seemed similar to the Blue Lagoon in tourist trap likeness. I would have loved to get out to sea at any fjord but it was not going to happen. Also, I would have loved to climb Kirkjufell.

I headed straight to Arkanes and the Gudlaug baths. These were free thermal baths that allowed people to get into the ocean! I dove in the 7° C water, swimming for several minutes. I explored the nearby jetty looking for dungeness crab but only found crab remnants. I also saw clear jellyfish. This was an amazing experience!

In the hot tub, I spoke with many people. One man used the Wim Hof method to stay in the water for nearly an hour. He trained every Wednesday morning. With cold water, my goal is to move around a lot to get my heart rate up. This activates adrenaline which fights off the cold. Then, when the sharp cold hits, I just accept. I feel instead of react.

This is like freediving, where once my chest starts to convulse for air, I simply feel. I am comfortable with 15 convulsions, each of which can be accepted, expanded to 2 seconds for a total of 30 additional seconds of down time. For me, this is taxing psychologically, so in the water, I come to the surface at that point, even though the body can allow many more convulsions.

On the other hand, in freediving quick breaths will make one's breath hold longer but debatably, will also cause shallow water blackouts. Raising the heart rate also causes shorter down time. In this freezing cold water, my down time dropped from 2 minutes to just 15 seconds, as I kept moving just to stay warm.

From there, I went to Galito to eat. The food was beautiful but this was my 3 star Google review for the $57 meal.

"Had the white chocolate langoustine soup which was a great start. I had the langoustine tagliatelle which was decent but maybe too heavy with the sauce and noodles. Finally, I had the fudge with raspberry sorbet. They were out of sorbet so I had pistachio ice cream instead. The dessert looked really pretty but I ate a few pieces of fudge and stuck to the ice cream. In other words, the meals went from best to worst. I kinda wish I just had a pizza and beer but the appetizer set off a different flow for the meal."

By the way, I stopped tipping early on in Iceland. I am accustomed to tipping 15 to 20 percent. I figure, if I am blessed enough to eat a meal out at a restaurant, I am blessed enough to also bless others. Even when taboo to tip, I find myself tipping. However, in Iceland, I stopped tipping after the first night.

Next, I went to Glymur, the second highest waterfall in Iceland. The hike was fun and includes a cool cave which I did not spend much time exploring.

This 3.4 km or 4.6 mile hike took me 1 hour and 21 minutes to complete at a steady 3.4 miles/hour pace. Taking that last selfie over the waterfall was scary since I am deathly afraid of heights!

I headed out in hopes of examining Iceland's sunset in a hot bath by the ocean. Taking intermittent dips and examining small schools of fish. I headed out to Nautholsvik Geothermal Park, right in Reykjavik. It closed earlier that day and the trickling water tempted me to dam up some areas to collect the water but I got the better of myself.

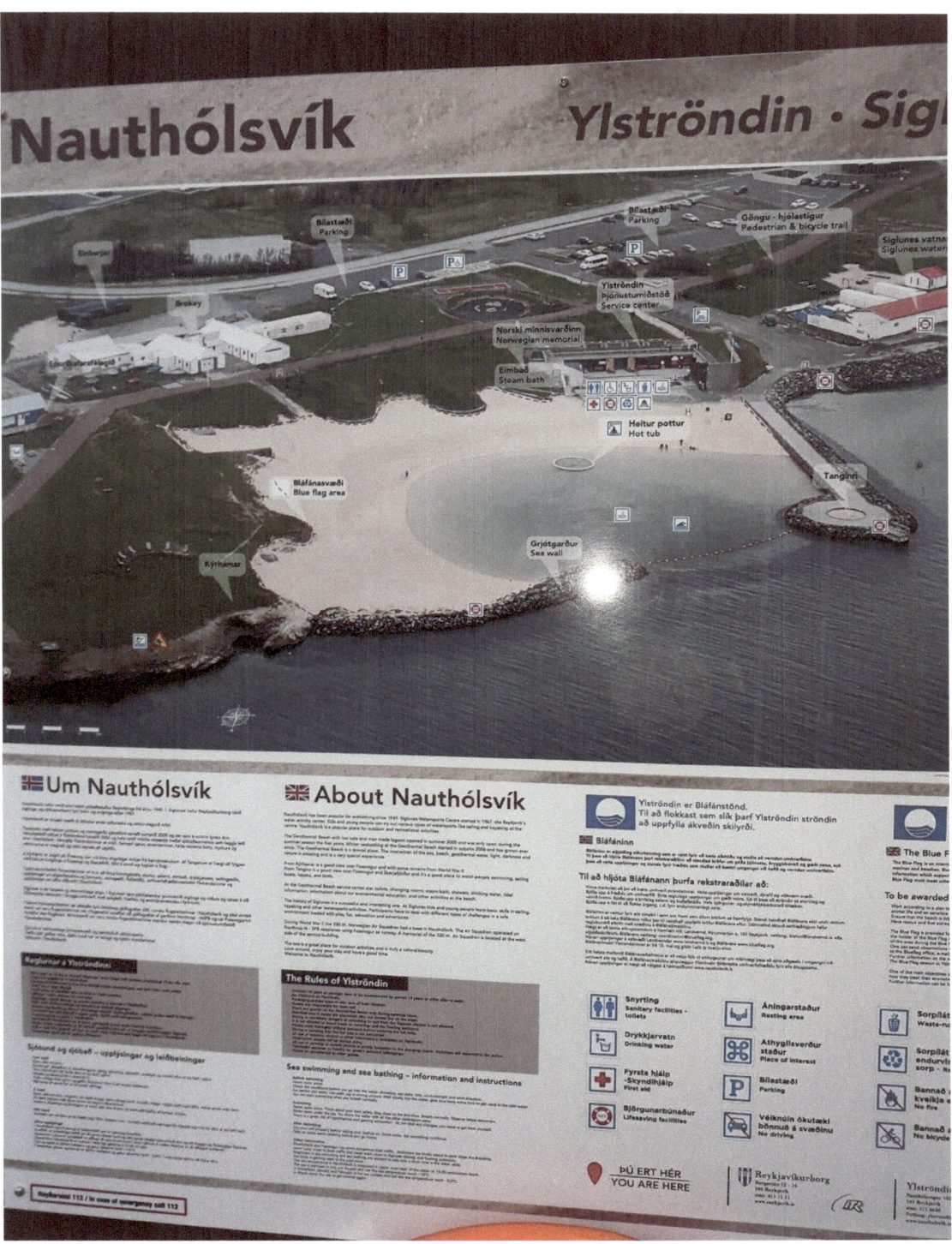

It was about midnight and I needed to return the car to the airport at 8:30am. Was this the end to my Iceland adventure? I felt I needed one last shenanigan.

I decided to head out to Reykjadular Thermal Baths.

← **Run**

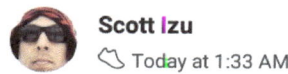

Scott Izu
Today at 1:33 AM

Reykjadalur Thermal River

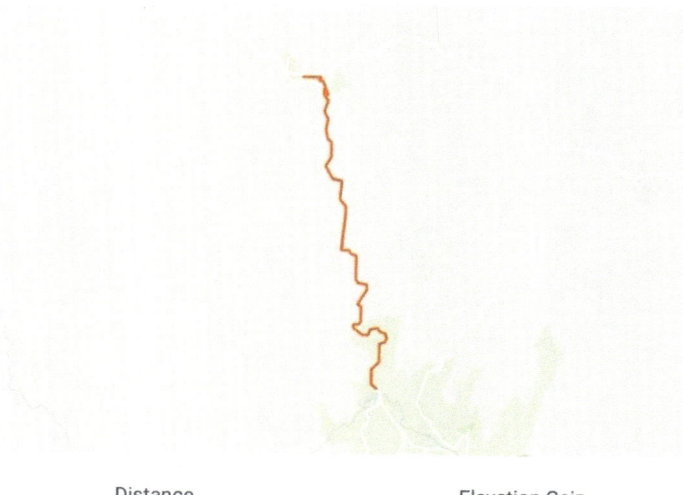

Distance	Elevation Gain
2.54 mi	813 ft

Moving Time	Avg Pace
57:18	22:32 /mi

Calories	Avg Heart Rate
659 cal	110 bpm

View Analysis

While I met several people along the hike up, I was just a lonely soul there at 3am. I enjoyed jumping in and out running from one end to the next. This bath is too cold, at the bottom. This bath is too hot, at the top. This bath is just right, in the middle. It was relaxing and I was only cold when I got out of the water. The water was only deep enough to lay down in. Any place deep enough to sit, collected too much water that had been allowed to cool down. The hottest water was on the surface, as it came immediately from further up the stream. They said many places were 100° C or boiling and had to be piped further away to hit 80° C.

Finally, I was ready to call it quits. I headed back to my car to rest a few hours before my flight. My final passage over the bridge at the entrance of the hike was met with several small fish collecting the nutrients.

Fish love where the current flows kicking up activity. I admired these fish and their relaxed free spirit which moved perfectly in sync with the current.

About the Author

Many people do not know I am divorced as it is hard for me to talk and answer questions about one of the most painful parts of my life. However, in the midst of pain, I found one of my greatest blessings. I read a book called Wild at Heart, which discusses a man's need for adventure, beauty and purpose.

I love adventure. As my physical body needs exercise, my spirit needs adventure. Without it, my soul weakens and slowly withers away. In a state of weakness, diseases such as pornography and gambling addictions creep in. Adventure is a key part of my recovery and helps me discover what it means to be a man.